MW00941938

Marian,

God loves you and
has a wonderful plan
for your life!

Jeremiah 29:11

Mrs. Slaughter

MESSAGES FROM MATTER

Finding God's Word in the Fundamentals of Chemistry

Sylvia Slaughter

WESTBOW
PRESS®
A DIVISION OF THOMAS NELSON
& ZONDERVAN

Scripture quotations taken from the New American
Standard Bible®, Copyright © 1960, 1962, 1963, 1968,
1971, 1972, 1973, 1975, 1977, 1995 by The Lockman
Foundation Used by permission." (www.Lockman.org)

WestBow Press books may be ordered through
booksellers or by contacting:

WestBow Press
A Division of Thomas Nelson & Zondervan
1663 Liberty Drive
Bloomington, IN 47403
www.westbowpress.com
1 (866) 928-1240

ISBN: 978-1-4908-9323-5 (sc)
ISBN: 978-1-4908-9324-2 (e)

Library of Congress Control Number: 2015913941

Print information available on the last page.

WestBow Press rev. date: 09/24/2015

For My Grandchildren

Contents

PREFACE

Since you have opened this little book and are reading this page you must be either a scientist or very brave! Or perhaps, hopefully, you are just overcome with curiosity. I encourage you to read on.

I have tried my best to write the science part of each topic in easy to understand language and to not go into too much technical detail. My husband, who has a Bachelor of Theology degree because it allowed him to opt-out of science courses, said it made sense to him. Other non-science readers ranging in age from teens to senior citizen status have echoed his thoughts.

So, even if you have always declared that science was your worst subject in school, read on. Read the chapters in the order they are arranged. Each one will prepare you for the next one. Most of all, do not try to read the whole book at once. Let the Lord open your mind and guide your thoughts. Who knows, you may even decide you like science!

In the words to Joshua, "Be strong and courageous! Do not tremble or be dismayed, for the LORD your God is with you wherever you go."

Sylvia Slaughter

January, 2010

Acknowledgements

If I had not received encouragement from friends and family I would never have been brave enough to see this little book through to the end. I would be remiss then if I did not thank them here.

Special thanks to:

Pauline Hall, a lovely and gracious Christian and retired teacher, for initially proofreading my manuscript and encouraging me to consider publishing it.

Nancy Herrington, an outstanding English teacher, and long time Christian friend and colleague, for reading, correcting, and offering constructive criticism on what became the final manuscript.

Sheila Carswell, computer teacher, for her word processing expertise.

Jeff Slaughter, husband, friend, Bible scholar, and my pastor for 38 years. He made sure that I was doctrinally correct, and he has been a source of continual support.

ROCKS

In the beginning God created everything that is, living and non-living alike. All creation exists to bring praise to Him. From the earliest days of man He has expected people to recognize His glory and to worship Him. His chosen people were commanded to be faithful in giving Him glory and to preach to all those who did not know the truth about the Creator of the universe.

Jesus says in Luke 19:40 if the praise of the people becomes silent the stones will cry out. Stones represent the inorganic, non-living matter in the universe. I believe the stones were designed from the beginning to call out the message of God. As the praise of people continues to diminish, the praise of the rocks continues to increase. Their cries first became apparent with the development of the study of chemistry in the 1700-1800's, but now are loud and clear for those who have ears to hear. With each new discovery the volume increases, so that even the hard of hearing might hear what God has to say.

God created all that exists from the smallest part of the atom to the largest galaxy, and because He did all matter must behave in a manner consistent with His character. Every property, every characteristic of all matter points to God to glorify Him. Matter cannot act contrarily to God's laws and plan for man because God is immutable and just in all His ways. Therefore, what applies to one part of creation must apply to all other parts of creation also. The behavior of matter parallels God's plan for the behavior of mankind.

This devotional book developed as I began to realize that the chemistry concepts I taught had spiritual applications. God's Word is not a science manual, but science books teach God's Word. I am learning that chemistry concepts provide Christian guidelines for every area of life and even illustrate the plan of salvation for non-believers.

I pray that these insights will encourage my Christian brothers and sisters to stand firm in the faith. I pray, too, that these words will convince some non-Christians to become believers. May we all have ears to hear what the rocks have to say.

SCIENTIFIC LAWS

Know therefore that the LORD your God, He is God, the faithful God, who keeps His covenant and His lovingkindness to a thousandth generation with those who love Him and keep His commandments; but repays those who hate Him to their faces, to destroy them; He will not delay with him who hates Him, He will repay him to his face. Deuteronomy 7:9-10

For truly I say to you, until heaven and earth pass away, not the smallest letter or stroke shall pass away from the Law, until all is accomplished. Matthew 5:18

Scientific laws describe universally applied results of actions. Some common laws include the Law of Definite Composition, the Law of Multiple Proportions, Avogadro's Law, Boyle's Law, Charles' Law, Newton's Law of Universal Gravitation, and the Laws of Motion. They explain what is true in any circumstance of nature. For example, the Law of Universal Gravitation describes the attractive force that exists between all objects in terms of the masses of the objects and the distance between them. Because the mass of the Earth is very large it exerts a strong attractive force on all objects that come close to it. Even the moon is attracted to the Earth, and in turn the Earth is attracted to the moon as evidenced by the oceans' tides. The law describes what happens but does not attempt to explain why or how these attractions occur. Trying to defy the Law of Gravity has consequences. Within the bounds of the gravitational forces on Earth the old saying, "What goes up must come down", is absolutely true. A person cannot deny its existence or say it does not apply to him. If he attempts to break the law he will suffer the consequence of falling toward the ground.

An important law in chemistry is the Law of Definite Composition, which says that one substance combines with another substance in exact proportions by mass. This means that every time those substances are combined in the same proportions the same product will be the result of the combination. For example, if hydrogen gas and oxygen gas are combined in a 1:8 proportion by mass, then water will be the resulting product. Failure to combine ingredients in proper amounts in any chemical reaction will result in a different product or a smaller amount of product and bits of left-over ingredients. In everyday life this law is illustrated when a person uses a recipe. Following the instructions exactly when making a cake will produce a delicious dessert. Failure to combine the ingredients in the correct amounts will result in an inferior product that might even be inedible.

God's laws operate in much the same way. He gave mankind some laws which He said must be obeyed. The first was to Adam and Eve when He told them not to eat the fruit of The Tree of the Knowledge of Good and Evil. He also told them the consequence of breaking that law. Eve was deluded by Satan into believing that she could successfully defy the law and brought about the consequence that exists even to today, the death of perfection.

God gave many other laws to fallen man to remind him what was right and wrong in his relationships with God and other people. Some were commands to individuals like Abraham when God told him to leave his home and family and travel to a new place. Others, like the Ten Commandments, were given to the nation of Israel. In all cases, God laid out His expectations including the rewards for keeping the laws and the consequences of the peoples' failure to live up to His expectations.

Jesus said that God's Laws would remain in force as long as we are living on this Earth. We are still obligated to keep His commandments and we must never forget that we will suffer in some way if we break them. Satan still tries to delude us into believing that we can successfully defy the laws of God. Often we fall into his trap. One day, however, God will finalize the consequence of breaking His Law by separating the lawbreakers from Him for all eternity. And this is what would happen to all of us, because we are all lawbreakers, except for the fact that Jesus came and suffered that separation from God in advance for us. It is Jesus and Jesus alone who allows us to receive "His lovingkindness to a thousandth generation".

Lord, help me to keep Your commandments and not be led astray. Thank You that I will not have to suffer the final consequence.

THEORIES

For who has known the mind of the Lord, that he should instruct Him? But we have the mind of Christ. I Corinthians 2:16

Ask, and it shall be given to you; seek, and you shall find; knock, and it shall be opened to you. Matthew 7:7

But know this first of all, that no prophecy of Scripture is a matter of one's own interpretation, for no prophecy was ever made by an act of human will, but men moved by the Holy Spirit spoke from God. 2 Peter 1:20-21

A scientific theory is an attempt to explain some aspect of the behavior of matter or energy. Theories are developed only after extensive study and experimentation. There are many named theories such as the Cell Theory, the Theory of Evolution, the Atomic Theory, the Kinetic-Molecular Theory, the Theory of Relativity, the Big Bang Theory, the Wave-Mechanical Theory, and the String Theory. All of them try to answer the question, "Why?" All of them are based on current experimental outcomes and analyses. This means all of them are subject to change as scientists gather new information from their research. If indisputable results arise from reliable experimentation which contradict a portion of a current theory then the theory is changed to reflect this new knowledge. So then, a theory is much more than a prediction or a hypothesis.

In everyday life people sometimes say, "I have a theory about that." when speaking of an idea that they have. This casual use of the term has led to skepticism of the accuracy and believability of scientific theories, but scientific theories are based on much more than whims and clever statements. They are the direct result of uncountable hours spent in a laboratory followed by in depth analysis of collected data. They are the outcome of the organized study of all aspects of the living and non-living world. Scientists recognize that even though they have learned a great deal about our universe much more is still waiting to be discovered. The result is the profound respect of the scientific community for the complexity of all that exists.

In much the same way, over the ages, people have tried to find explanations for many other aspects of life such as good fortune, bad fortune, life, death, and the after-life. Their ideas have ranged from wild and improbable to logical and plausible. Some are a result of creative imaginations out of which came stories of strange creatures, gods, and goddesses known today as Mythology. These have long ago ceased to be anything but good stories. They have been replaced by some equally wild and improbable theories of alien invasions and mysterious, but missing races of people. Added to these ideas are the predictions of astrology and palmistry and the power of crystals and pyramids, which many people consider logical and plausible answers to questions.

Secular Humanism rejects all those notions and seeks to find its answers within man's mind alone.

God does not intend for us to seek for answers alone. Since the beginning all anyone has had to do is ask Him for help in finding a solution to a problem or an explanation for an event. He will reveal answers as we are ready to hear and understand them. This includes explanations for both scientific and non-scientific questions. If our explanations do not agree with what is in God's Word we must continue to investigate and be willing to modify our theories accordingly. A woman once said to her pastor after his sermon, "Are you telling me I have been wrong about this my whole life?" He found out she had never checked to see what the Bible had to say.

The Bible itself has many examples of how men's ideas changed as God revealed more information to them. In the book of Job, while it begins with a conversation between God and Satan, Job does not appear to have a concept of Satan as a source of evil; but by the time of Jesus many ideas about the devil and his demons had emerged. Our current explanation of the evil that exists in us and in the world is based on the analysis of data found in the scriptures. Any concept of Satan, whether it comes from an individual or from an organized religion, contrary to what is presented in the Bible must be rejected and their concepts must be modified to conform to reflect the truths revealed to the inspired writers of God's Word.

Many theories such as those about the abode of the dead, the second coming of Christ, why good people suffer, faith and healing, angels, and life after death exist today. What Christians must do is compare all that they read and hear with what is revealed in the Bible about these things. We can never tell God what is right or even presume to know everything there is to know about a topic. We do, however, have the "mind of Christ" so if we commune with God He can and will reveal His Word to us through His Holy Spirit. Our response, like that of the scientists, will be a profound respect for the complexity of all that exists.

Lord, guide me as I seek to find Your truth in all things and give me the courage to change my theories to match Your revelations to me.

CONSERVATION
OF MASS

17

In the beginning God created the heavens and the earth. Then God blessed the seventh day and sanctified it, because in it He rested from all His work which God had created and made. Genesis 1:1, 2:3

He is before all things, and in Him all things hold together. Colossians 1:17

Then I saw a new heaven and a new earth; for the first heaven and the first earth passed away. Revelation 21:1

The Law of Conservation of Mass says that mass (matter) cannot be created or destroyed, but its form can be changed. This is the fundamental law of chemistry. Along with the Law of Conservation of Energy, this law is the foundation for all changes and reactions of matter, physical, chemical, and nuclear. The word *create* means to produce something from nothing, that is to bring matter into existence. It is different from the word *make* which simply means to use already existing matter to form something new. The total amount of mass of the substances present at the beginning of a change is equal to the total amount of mass of the products which result. For example, in the physical change of freezing the mass of liquid water used to make ice will be the same as the mass of the ice cubes that result. If a balloon is placed over the top of a container to capture the gas then the total mass of the baking soda and vinegar before they are combined will be the same as the total mass of the carbon dioxide gas and the remaining substances in the container after the chemical change is complete. Even in nuclear reactions, which involve changes in radioactive elements, mass is conserved. The Law of Conservation of Energy which states that energy cannot be created or destroyed is important in understanding nuclear reactions. Seemingly, on occasion, mass appears to be destroyed in certain nuclear reactions. However, scientists have discovered that energy appears as mass disappears. Einstein is credited with the formula $E = mc^2$ which accurately describes the rate at which mass can become energy and energy can be converted into mass. Scientists do not all agree about the origin of matter and energy, but they do agree that the total amount of matter and energy in the universe is constant. They know that humans cannot create or destroy mass.

Christians know that it is God who created the matter and energy that exists throughout the universe. He is the One who then made everything by using His created materials. God is now resting from his creative activity. His Son is the One who holds it all together so that nothing can be destroyed. God, the creator and sustainer of the entire universe, has given us the knowledge to use and change His creations, and with this knowledge to recognize our inability to do what He alone can do.

Only God can cause things to exist and only God can cause them to pass out of existence. Everything is totally in His hands to do with as He pleases. Only God can destroy, but He has chosen not to destroy. He blessed His creative work and called it good. Because it is good, God will abide by His own Law of Conservation until the end of time as we know it. When He calls us to enter into eternity with Him, He is going to produce a new heaven and a new Earth from the old heaven and Earth. We will be the recipients of a new home made from the greatest physical, chemical, and nuclear changes ever devised. Jesus will continue to hold it together. Then all people from all the ages will have to acknowledge the Source of all that exists for all eternity.

Lord, I praise You for the goodness of Your creation and the opportunity to praise You forever.

THE ATOMIC
THEORY

Through faith we understand that the worlds were framed by the word of God, so that things which are seen were not made of things which do appear. But without faith it is impossible to please him: for he that cometh to God must believe that He is, and that He is a rewarder of them that diligently seek Him. Hebrews 11: 3, 6

The Atomic Theory has been discussed, debated, ignored, analyzed, changed, and adjusted for over 2000 years. The Greek philosopher Democritus began it all with his idea that it might just be possible to cut something in half over and over until an undividable piece of that something was attained. He called that piece *atomos* which meant indivisible. Mostly, he was laughed at, and when he died so did his idea. Amazingly, his writings survived and John Dalton revived his idea in the early 1800's. Dalton proclaimed that all matter was made of tiny, indivisible particles called atoms. This time around the idea was lauded as the absolute answer to the mysteries of nature. The study of the chemical properties of matter was popular throughout Europe and Dalton's Atomic Theory explained many of the previously unexplainable phenomena. All was well in the scientific world---until the late 1800's when

J.J. Thomson, Ernest Rutherford, and others discovered that Dalton was wrong. The atom could be divided! Protons, electrons, neutrons, positrons, beta particles, and more were identified. Now scientists know that protons and neutrons can be broken down into smaller particles called quarks, and some evidence exists that quarks are composed of even smaller bits of matter. Today's nuclear scientists are realizing that they are still a long way from understanding the atom, and that the analysis has just begun. Their work is cut out for them. They are ready. They are excited. They want to know all they can possibly know.

Many persons behave toward God as the Greeks did toward the idea of the atom. They do not understand God so they ignore Him and try to pretend He does not exist. God will not cease to exist any more than the atom ceased to exist simply because people said it did not.

Others act like Dalton. Thinking that God is fairly simple to explain, they box Him up in a neat little package. It is when we think that we know everything there is to know that we need to be the most careful. If we know all there is to know about God then we are dangerously close to declaring ourselves gods.

We must be careful, as Christians, to study God in the same way the chemists of today study the atom. We must know that we do not understand Him fully. We must be ready, excited, and wanting to learn as much as we possibly can about the nature of God. Just as the persistence of scientists has yielded more and more knowledge of the atom, so God will reward our persistence by revealing more and more of Himself to us.

> *Lord, I pray that I will be infinitely more eager to know You than the chemist is to know the atom.*

ATOMIC FORCES

And in Him all things hold together. He is also head
of the body, the church. Colossians 1:17b, 18a

A toms are divided into two parts, the nucleus and the electron cloud. The nucleus consists of positively charged protons and uncharged neutrons. The electron cloud contains negatively charged electrons, equal in number to the protons in a particular nucleus, each spinning around the nucleus in its own individual path and giving the atom an approximately spherical shape.

Both electrical forces and nuclear forces act on the atom. The electrical force causes like charges to repel each other and opposite charges to attract each other. This force acting alone would result in the break-up of the atom. The positively charged protons, which are closely packed in the nucleus, would repel each other strongly and the negatively charged electrons would collapse into the nucleus as a result of their attraction to the protons. Fortunately, the nuclear forces also act, in ways not completely understood, to hold the nucleus together and to keep the electrons in their paths.

As Christians, many forces like the electrical forces in the atom affect us. We often find ourselves at odds with other Christians. We move away from each other putting as much distance as possible between us and those with whom we have so much in common. We are attracted to persons and ideas that are completely opposite to us. We are attracted to the world. This attraction is as destructive to the church as the electrical force alone would be destructive to the atom.

Jesus is our nuclear force. Ultimately, it is He, the creator of the atom itself, who holds the atomic particles in place. So then, it must be He, the creator of the Church, who holds and preserves the body of Christ. He alone will hold us together in harmony when we would attempt to be separated. He alone will keep the world from collapsing in on us. He alone will preserve us from total destruction. He alone will allow us to continue firmly established and steadfast in our faith.

> *Lord, help us to understand that You and You alone hold the universe, from galaxies to atoms, together. In this understanding give us confidence that You can also hold the Church together.*

NUCLIDES

For just as we have many members in one body and all the members do not have the same function, so we, who are many, are one body in Christ. Romans 12:4-5

After these things I looked, and behold, a great multitude, which no one could count, from every nation and all tribes and peoples and tongues standing before the throne and before the Lamb. Revelation 7:9

Chemists use the term nuclide to describe individual forms of atoms of the elements. Ninety-two elements exist in nature but there are hundreds of nuclides. All atoms with the same number of protons are atoms of the same element. Not all the atoms of an element are identical, however, as they may contain varying numbers of neutrons. In fact, all the natural elements have one or more isotopes, a term used to describe the individual nuclides of a particular element. The slight variation in atomic particle content often is accompanied by a variation in the properties of the nuclide. The change may be slight and virtually unnoticeable under most conditions, or it may be a radical, quite pronounced change in properties. These variations can be used by chemists to produce specific compounds for special uses. Sometimes the nuclide itself can be used in a special way. For instance, hydrogen has three isotopes. Hydrogen-1 is the most common form making up over ninety-nine percent of all the hydrogen that exists. Hydrogen-2, or Deuterium, is used to make what is called "heavy water". Heavy water is used as a tracer in physiology research and as a moderator in nuclear reactors, but it cannot be substituted for ordinary water as drinking water. Hydrogen-3, or tritium, is radioactive, and is used in nuclear weapons and in fusion research.

Christians are like the nuclides. They are all alike in that they are all human beings just as nuclides are all forms of elements; but they come from all walks of life, from all races and nationalities, and have a variety of gifts, talents, and personalities. God recognizes these differences, however great or small, and has a use for each Christian that is specific, and for whom there is no substitute. He has already given each Christian his spiritual gifts and has a plan of "good works" designed for him. Just as chemists recognize, appreciate, and use the diversity among the elements, so Christians need to recognize, appreciate, and use their diversities. In doing so, they will complete the body of Christ on earth and prepare themselves for the completion of the body of Christ in Heaven.

> *Lord, thank You for creating me a special and unique individual. May I come to see the same joy in diversity as You do.*

THE NOBLE
GASES

Therefore you are to be perfect, as your heavenly Father is perfect. Matthew 5:48

I and the Father are one. John 10:30

Beloved, now we are children of God, and it has not appeared as yet what we shall be. We know that, when He appears, we shall be like Him, because we shall see Him as He is. I John 3:2

The electron structure of an atom is of utmost importance in determining its chemical reactivity. Chemists have proven that the complete number of outer shell electrons is eight. All chemical reactions between atoms are a result of the atoms' attempts to obtain complete outer energy levels by sharing or transferring their electrons. Nearly all the atoms that exist are chemically active; that is, they have outer shells containing less than eight electrons. A very few atoms (neon, argon, krypton, xenon, and radon) have exactly eight electrons in their outer shells. Helium is complete with two electrons in its one energy level. These six elements do not react chemically either with themselves or with atoms of other elements. There is no need, for they are already complete as they are. They are, so to speak, perfect atoms and are generally referred to as the Noble Gases.

Jesus is like the Noble Gases. He, too, is complete and perfect. He is completely God and completely man. He is noble, the King of Kings and the Lord of Lords. He has set the standard by which all humans must measure themselves.

Human beings are like the other atoms. When we measure ourselves physically, spiritually, socially, and emotionally, we find that we are lacking something. Our lifetimes are spent trying to find perfection in these areas. We attempt to rid ourselves of bad habits and then the accompanying guilt when we are not successful. We are constantly trying to somehow convince others, ourselves, and even God that we are of worth. As Romans 3:23 states, we "have all sinned and come short of the glory of God."

As Christians we have, through Jesus, God's approval. Even so, we are not automatically made perfect. Sin is still a part of our lives and must be dealt with constantly. We still struggle with feelings of inadequacy and guilt. We still have the desire to be approved by others, ourselves, and God. We continue to need God's forgiveness for our imperfections.

But, praise God, we will not always be like the atoms with incomplete energy levels! We Christians have the promise from God that one day we will be like Jesus, complete and perfect in every way. We too will be noble, and will reign with Him forever!

> *Lord, thank You for the hope of glory, and for the knowledge that we shall one day be like You.*

DIATOMIC
MOLECULES

*But now having been freed from sin and enslaved to
God, you derive your benefit, resulting in sanctification,
and the outcome, eternal life. Romans 6:22*

The active gases are hydrogen, nitrogen, oxygen,
fluorine, chlorine, bromine, and iodine. Bromine
and iodine are actually a liquid and a solid,
respectively, at room temperature, but much of their
behavior is similar to their gaseous relatives, fluorine
and chlorine. Some of these elements are found free
in nature. In fact, nitrogen and oxygen alone make up
about ninety-nine percent of our atmosphere. The others
can be separated from compounds and bottled as pure
elements. None of these elements exist as single atoms.
In order to be free each must be bonded to another atom
of the same element. Two atoms of oxygen are bonded
together, two atoms of hydrogen, two atoms of fluorine,
and so on, as diatomic molecules. If ever the bond that
makes them free is broken, then immediately, they will
be captured by atoms of some other element and will
form bonds that will cause them to lose their identities
as elements.

Not all these elements are bonded equally. Hydrogen,
fluorine, chlorine, bromine, and iodine have only a single
bond to hold the two atoms together. Two bonds hold a

pair of oxygen atoms and three bonds hold two nitrogen atoms. The more bonds that hold the atoms together, the less likely it is that they will be broken apart. That is the primary reason that nitrogen gas makes up seventy-eight percent of the atmosphere. It does not easily make itself available to other elements.

As Christians our freedom is measured by the strength of our bonds of prayer, Bible study, and a desire to do God's will. When our bonds are secure, we exist free in nature. Others can easily identify us as Christians. Many of us are content to be single bond Christians to make and break our relationship with the Lord. We want to be free, but see little harm in joining with the unsaved world. We are still Christians, but our true nature is hidden. Our identities as Christians are gone. We appear to be something else. Instead, our goal should be to choose to live as triple-bond believers. We would stand free and pure, a strong and measurable influence in the world, just as nitrogen is a strong, measurable factor in the atmosphere.

Lord, I want to experience the freedom to be found in You as Your slave. Bind me ever closer to You.

POLYATOMIC
IONS

45

As obedient children do not be conformed to the former lusts which were yours in you ignorance, but like the Holy One who called you, be holy yourselves also in all your behavior. 1 Peter 1:14-15

Polyatomic ions are groups of two or more atoms which have combined together by sharing electrons, but which also have an electrical charge. When most atoms share electrons with each other, they do so in such a way to eliminate any excess positive or negative charges. The product, the new substance formed, is electrically neutral. Polyatomic ions are essentially new substances because the bonds between the atoms are so strong that the group acts as though it were a single atom. However, these ions still need one or more electrons to become electrically neutral. They are chemically incomplete. They will always combine with atoms that are able to give them the electrons they need.

As Christians, we tend to be like polyatomic ions. We have combined our lives with Jesus. We are new creatures in Christ. There are, however, some areas of our lives that we are unwilling to give to Him. We want to keep some parts for ourselves just as the polyatomic ions keep some unshared electrons. We know that we are incomplete.

Consciously or unconsciously we are always searching for some way to fill in the gaps in our lives. Each time the thought, "I want to do it my way," comes to mind there is the evidence of another unshared bond. We have the desire to combine with something in the world to eliminate the empty places. For a Christian, however, there is no sense of real satisfaction in these worldly bonds even when they are represented by altruistic deeds. At times these bonds produce destructive personal behavior and relationships. The goal of every Christian should be to replace the "my way" with "Jesus' way" in all things, to be complete in Him and Him alone.

Lord, help me to want to exchange my former desires for the one desire to be holy and complete in You.

METALLIC BONDS

A new commandment I give to you, that you love one another, even as I have loved you, that you also love one another. By this all men will know that you are My disciples, if you have love for one another. John 13:34-35

And all those who had believed were together, and had all things in common; and they began selling their property and possessions, and were sharing them with all, as anyone might have need. Acts 2:44-45

...standing firm in one spirit, with one mind striving together for the faith of the gospel; Phil. 1:27

Metallic bonding differs from metal-nonmetal (ionic bonds) and nonmetal-nonmetal (covalent) bonds in the way the electrons are distributed. In both ionic and covalent bonds the outermost electrons are transferred or shared between two specific atoms, but in metallic bonds the outer electrons are free to move from one atom to another in what is often called a "sea of electrons". These free roaming electrons do not belong to any one particular atom and can travel anywhere in the piece of metal. The properties of metals result from this electron arrangement. Metals are excellent absorbers and reflectors of light.

The electrons absorb many frequencies of light and then immediately release the light energy which gives metals their luster. Another property is malleability which means that a metal can be hammered or rolled into thin sheets without breaking. Ductility is the property that allows metals to be squeezed through small openings to form wires. They are also excellent conductors of electricity and heat. If metals are rapidly and repeatedly heated and cooled in the same place they become brittle and will break at that spot, but careful melting can weld the parts together again.

The Christians of the early church bonded together in a unique way similar to the way metals bond. No matter who they were before Christ entered their lives, they were alike in Him. They felt this so strongly that they were willing to share everything with everyone. Possessions were distributed from person to person much as electrons flow from atom to atom in metals. This tied them together so strongly that they did not want to part from one another as seen by the fact that they met and worshipped all day every day.

The early Christians were malleable. The persecutors could beat them and bend them but not break them. Their response was to meet and pray, to send money to those in need, and to rejoice in their trials because they knew that the bond would hold no matter what the test. The first Christians were also ductile. As persecutions persisted they were scattered across the known world, drawn out by God, but never truly separated from one another. The bonds held as was evidenced by the shared letters and the individuals sent to visit the various churches that kept springing up. They loved and cared for one another so much that no matter how much they were pulled and stretched, they never lost the sense of being one entity.

In all these ways the church showed Jesus to the world. They absorbed the love of Christ when they were saved and then immediately released it so that everyone they came in contact with could see the "light of the world". Because Satan hates the Light, he stepped in to try to break apart the early church. Heated arguments and frosty responses weakened the church in places. Lies, complaints, and dissentions produced the first fragments. Prayers and God's grace brought them back together again.

As it was then, so it is today. We still reach out to each other in Christian love, but we have been separated by Satan. Each fragmented part still functions as a metal. We try to show love and care within our groups, but there are many limitations to our success in sharing the love of God with the lost. We have become mere pinpoints of light. Imagine how it would be, if through prayer and God's grace, we could all be welded together again into one great sheet of metal reflecting the light of His love to the dark world.

> *Lord, forgive us for allowing the petty divisions caused by Satan to separate us from our brothers and sisters in Christ. Rekindle in us the love the early Christians had for each other. Bind us together again.*

THE PERIODIC
TABLE

For where jealousy and selfish ambition exist, there is disorder and every evil thing. James 3:10

God is not a god of confusion but of peace, as in all the churches of the saints. Let all things be done properly and in an orderly manner. 1 Corinthians 14:33, 40

A few hundred years ago when the science of chemistry was just beginning only a few elements were identified. Various symbols were assigned to them but they were not categorized in any particular way. As more elements were discovered some small attempts at arranging them were made; but it was not until about sixty-three elements had been found that anyone recognized that there was a real need for an orderly arrangement of some sort. Dimitri Mendeleev, a Russian chemist, found that by comparing the atomic masses of the elements that many could be arranged into groups possessing similar properties. This first periodic table had gaps in it. Mendeleev predicted that these gaps would be filled with undiscovered elements, and he even predicted their properties. Within a few years his predictions came true. About fifty years later Henry Moseley discovered a better way to arrange the elements. New information about atoms and better technology allowed him to identify the number of protons in the atoms of each element now called the atomic number of the element. When he rearranged the table according to the increasing atomic numbers of the elements he found that all the elements with similar physical and chemical properties lined up in vertical columns perfectly. This form of the table is still used today.

If nothing else, the periodic arrangement of the elements shows that God is orderly and purposeful. Such perfect order cannot be the result of mere accident. He is not a god of chance and chaos. Instead He is the God of creation, the planner and arranger of all matter in the universe. If we do not perceive order in all things, it is not because it is not there, but simply that we have not discovered it as yet, just as the early chemists did not recognize the order of the elements. God is perfect in all things, and so His creation must be also.

In addition, however, there is an application of the concept of order to the church. The church is not to be a haphazard collection of activities, a chaos out of which little of value comes. It is also not to be a place of bickering and fighting, with each Christian trying to occupy the same position. Instead, Christians have their own individual gifts, which give them their own personal place for service. When Christians in a local church are serving in their proper places, gaps in places of ministry will sometimes be found. Just as God allowed chemists to discover the missing elements to fill in the gaps in the periodic table, He will provide the church with persons to fill the ministry gaps. Only when we are willing to follow God's orderly plan will we see progress in ministry and peace in the church.

Lord, thank You for the peace we find in following Your plan.

CHANGES

Therefore if any man is in Christ, he is a new creature; the old things passed away, behold, new things have come. 2 Corinthians 5:16

Chemistry is the study of the composition of matter and the changes that can occur in matter. Chemists are particularly interested in two types of changes that take place, physical changes and chemical changes.

Physical changes are those in which the identifying properties of substances remain unchanged. Physical changes include changes in the state, size or shape of matter. No matter what changes occur, the nature of the substance remains the same. It can be boiled or frozen, molded, sculpted, or pulverized; but no real change in the substance itself takes place. For example, water may be heated to form steam or cooled to form ice. As a solid it may be in the form of cubes, used to make beautiful ice sculptures, or served as crushed ice. But it never stops being water.

Chemical changes are those in which new substances with new properties are formed. Changes occur which alter the composition of the matter itself. A simple illustration of this type of change is the reaction between hydrogen and oxygen to produce water. Hydrogen is a gas which burns. Oxygen is a gas that supports combustion. A chemical change occurs when these two gases combine. The product is very unlike either of the two original substances. It is water, which is a liquid at ordinary room temperature, and which neither burns nor supports combustion.

Many people spend their lives, and their money, seeking to improve themselves with physical changes. The boiling, freezing, molding, sculpting, and pulverizing of their bodies and minds occupy their every waking moment. They believe that brand-name clothes, new hairstyles, expensive cosmetics, certain scents of colognes and aftershaves, various diet foods and pills, gym memberships, and stacks of self-help books will turn them into the persons they always wanted to be, admired by one and all. Each one says, "I just want to make myself a better person." No matter what they do, though, they are still the same persons they were before the changes took place. When the makeup comes off and the mind molding exercises wear thin it is easy to see that the composition of the material is not changed.

The only way a person can really change is to be willing to react, to combine with Christ. This results in a change like a chemical change in matter. A new person with new characteristics is actually formed. The old properties are gone and new properties have taken their place. A new creature in Christ is the result when a person is saved. Outwardly, this person may appear to be the same as always, but inwardly he will be completely different. Jesus combines totally with all parts of a human's personality so that truly the old is passed away and all things are made new.

Lord, forgive me for my personal efforts to give myself a makeover. Change me completely as only You can.

PHYSICAL
EQUILIBRIUM

Does the Lord take delight in thousands of rams, in ten thousand rivers of oil? Shall I present my first-born for my rebellious acts, the fruit of my body for the sin of my soul? Micah 6:7

Because by the works of the Law, no flesh will be justified in His sight; for through the Law comes the knowledge of sin. Romans 3:20

Always learning and never able to come to the knowledge of the truth. 2 Timothy 3:7

For by grace you have been saved…not as a result of works, so that no one may boast. Ephesians 2:8-9

Whenever a chemist seeks to cause a change, a state of equilibrium may result. Equilibrium is a state of balance between a forward and a backward change. With physical equilibrium no chemical changes occur, that is, the beginning substances are also the ending substances. The changes that do occur are physical changes. For instance, when sugar granules are placed in a container of water they will begin to dissolve. The particles will separate and spread out evenly in the water. At some point in the process the sugar particles will begin to rejoin to form larger sugar grains again. When the dissolving and reforming occurs at an equal rate then equilibrium is reached. If more water is added to the mixture the balance is upset and more sugar will again begin to dissolve until equilibrium is re-established. No matter what point in the process samples are taken the only two substances which will be observed in the container are sugar and water.

The evaporation-condensation process is another example of physical equilibrium. Water will evaporate until equal amounts of water vapor and liquid water exist in a container. When a person works outside on a dry day his perspiration will evaporate rapidly into the atmosphere. However, on a humid day the perspiration will for the most part remain on his skin. The equilibrium point is quickly established as the air becomes saturated with water vapor.

Many people are seeking to establish an acceptable state of equilibrium in their lives. They want to reach a point where they feel comfortable and content. They believe that they are neither bad nor good but hope that the good somewhat outweighs the bad. When they think they have done something detrimental to this state of balance they perform a good deed or kind act of some sort to swing the equilibrium of their lives back in the positive direction. Some believe if they dedicate their entire lives to good causes and philanthropic organizations, or to becoming outstanding, foremost authorities in their chosen field, they will be assured a place of honor for all time.

Unfortunately, these good and bad deeds do not result in a real change in the container. Like the sugar water example, no matter how the mixture is adjusted the materials remain the same. Equilibrium will always be re-established. Good works will never permanently triumph over bad works. Throughout time God has rejected people on the basis of their works alone. Attempting to perfectly keep the law only shows them how futile the attempt is. The more they try to follow the rules the more they are aware of the sin in their lives. The more they are aware of the sin, the harder they try to follow the rules. They are in a state of equilibrium from which they cannot escape on their own. Only God Himself can change the container and its contents.

Lord, help me to grieve over the lives of those who are caught in the never ending cycle of trying to measure up on their own.

SYNTHESIS
REACTIONS

For this cause a man shall leave his father and his mother, and shall cleave to his wife; and they shall become one flesh. Genesis 2:24

That they may all be one; even as Thou, Father, art in Me, and I in Thee, that they also may be in Us; that the world may believe that Thou didst send Me. John 17:21

No one shall snatch them out of My hand…no one is able to snatch them out of the Father's hand. John 10:28-29

Synthesis means to put things together in order to produce something new. In chemical terms it involves taking elements and/or simple compounds and joining them to form a different substance, larger and more complex than the original substances. In all cases two or more substances become one new substance. The properties of the new compound are different from the properties of the original elements or compounds. Sometimes a synthesis reaction uses only two elements, combines them chemically, and makes a compound. For instance, sodium metal plus chlorine gas produces sodium chloride which is known as salt. The properties of common table salt are certainly different from the properties of the elements which make it up. It is also possible to make new compounds composed of hundreds or even thousands of other simple compounds. The organic compounds found in living things - complex carbohydrates, lipids, and proteins - are examples of these types of compounds. Many plastics such as polyethylene are made of a thousand or more simple gaseous petroleum compounds combined chemically.

It is difficult to break chemical compounds apart. Once the chemical reactions have occurred they cannot be separated by ordinary means. The bonds between the elements are strong and only another chemical reaction can bring about a change. One element is pulled away from the other, thus destroying the bond.

The idea of unity, of becoming one, is an essential concept for Christians. From the beginning God illustrated this with His words to Adam and Eve in the Garden of Eden. Marriage is to be a joining together of separate individuals in such a way as to produce one new, more complex unit with different characteristics. Ideally, a married couple plans as one, thinks as one, and acts as one. Jesus said in reference to marriage that men should not seek to break apart what God has put together. Sometimes people allow another chemical reaction to tear their marriages apart. These reactions result from many different outside influences, but the cause and effect is the same. One person is pulled away and the marriage bond is broken.

Another synthesis reaction occurs when a person unites his life with Christ. Christ lives in him and he lives in Christ. A Christian is a new creature with new characteristics. This is the first and simplest type of synthesis God planned to reunite men to Him. Jesus said He was in the Father and the Father in Him. Christians have Jesus living in them and therefore the Father lives in them, too. Because God is omnipresent then all Christians everywhere are bonded together in a second and more complex type of synthesis. The relationship between Christians is unique. It is stronger than any relationships between or with non-Christians. Sometimes Christians allow outside influences to pull them away from each other, but a bond between Christians can never truly be broken. Neither can the bond between God and the Christian. It is a promise that Jesus made to his disciples. Synthesis with God is eternal.

Lord, thank You for your strong hold on me. Help me to cling to You and to my fellow believers in the same way.

DECOMPOSITION
REACTIONS

And let men call on God earnestly that each may turn from his wicked way and from the violence which is in his hands. Jonah 3:8

Now therefore, make confession to the Lord God of your fathers and do His will; and separate yourselves from the peoples of the land and from the foreign wives. Ezra 10:11

Peter began to say to Him, "Behold, we have left everything and followed You." Mark 10:28

Decomposition reactions are chemical reactions that result in the separation of more complex compounds into less complex compounds and elements. The chemical bond between the substances is broken so that the particles can exist free in nature or can form other bonds. Most elements are chemically active and tend to form bonds with other elements. The presence of these individual elements is hidden by the bond because the bonding produces a new substance with new properties. It was not until men understood this that many elements were discovered. For instance, most metals are bonded to non-metals in nature so that their properties are hidden. It was not until men learned to break those bonds that iron, copper, aluminum, and many other metals were found. Today the science of metallurgy involves extensive knowledge of decomposition reactions. The decay of dead plants and animals is another example of decomposition which releases substances from their bonds so that they can be reused in new ways. Even the digestive process is composed of several decomposition reactions which break down food into simple substances useful to the organism.

Throughout the ages God has called his people to separate themselves. As one element tends to form a bond with another element rather than exist free in nature, so do people tend to form bonds with other people, things, and activities. Non-Christians are permanently bonded to sin, and must undergo a decomposition reaction called repentance as a first step to salvation. They must free themselves from their wicked activities by calling on God to take their sin away so that they can recombine with Him. God's people must also be careful about forming alliances with questionable groups. Sometimes Christians become so involved and tied up in the world they form bonds that leave God out, perhaps with the best of intentions, but always with disastrous results. Christians need to recognize when they are involved in unhealthy relationships and be willing to break away from those relationships. The Christian's usefulness to God is often defined by the extent to which he is willing to release himself from his ties to the world. Every Christian's goal should be to be able to say as Peter did, "Behold, we have left everything and followed You."

Lord, help me to recognize the things I need to let go of for the sake of following You.

SINGLE
DISPLACEMENT
REACTIONS

When a strong man, fully armed, guards his own house, his possessions are undisturbed. But when someone stronger than he attacks him and overpowers him, he takes away from him all his armor on which he had relied and distributes his plunder. Luke 11:21-22

Greater is He who is in you than he who is in the world. I John 4:4

It is to your advantage that I go away; for if I do not go away, the Helper will not come to you; but if I go, I will send Him to you. John 16:7

And the devil who deceived them was thrown into the lake of fire and brimstone…and will be tormented day and night forever and ever. Rev. 20:10

Single displacement reactions involve a chemical compound and a free element. The free element is more active than one of the elements in the compound and is able to replace that less active element in the compound. A more active metal will replace a less active metal or a more active non-metal will replace a less active non-metal. If the metal zinc is placed in a solution of the compound copper sulfate, the zinc will remove the copper and take its place. The result would be copper metal in a zinc sulfate solution. The non-metal chlorine is more active than the non-metal iodine. Therefore, chlorine would react with the compound sodium iodide to produce sodium chloride and the element iodine. The relative activities of metals and non-metals have been made into charts for chemists to consult. Any element that is listed higher on the chart is capable of displacing an element that is lower on the list. It is important that the free element be left in the solution until the reaction is complete because most reactions are not instantaneous. The greater the difference in the reactivity of the two elements the quicker the reaction will take place.

Every year when January arrives people like to make resolutions. They want to replace a bad habit with a good habit – sitting on the couch all evening with exercise, nail biting with manicures, junk food with healthy snacks or procrastination with productivity. These resolutions are met with varying levels of success depending on how consistently they work at carrying them out. The good habit must be constantly applied in order to displace the bad habit. If it is not, the bad habit will persist and will sometimes become even worse. Jesus said in Luke 11:24-26 that unless the demon which was cast out is replaced, it will come back with friends and make matters worse than ever.

This scripture applies not only to the idea of New Year's resolutions but also to the popular idea that people can apply self-help techniques to make themselves into ideal individuals. Just as an element cannot replace itself in a single displacement reaction, so humans cannot replace themselves through human activity. They must be careful in thinking they are in control over their lives because Satan is always ready to take over with his superior strength.

Non-Christians are controlled by Satan in everything they do and think even though they are probably not aware of his presence. The most important decision they can make is to allow Jesus to come into their lives and displace Satan. This is the ultimate single displacement reaction. God is greater than Satan so once God lives in them Satan can never come back. He can live in close proximity with Christians and attempt to influence them but he cannot ever displace the presence of God in their lives.

During the time period between the first time Jesus was on earth and when He is coming back to be with all Christians forever, another single displacement reaction took place, the one which resulted in the coming of the Holy Spirit as the replacement for the physical presence of Jesus. The presence of the Holy Spirit serves as a constant reminder to Christians that they are combined with the most reactive and therefore irreplaceable being. Finally, when Christ does come back and establish His Kingdom and Christians are in the presence of God eternally, one last single displacement reaction will occur. God will take His place in the new Heaven and the new Earth and displace forever the presence of evil. The devil and all unsaved people will be separated everlastingly into the lake of fire. God will wipe away the last tear and Christians will live in perfection in life without end.

Lord, I thank You for the single displacement reaction that has guaranteed me life eternal with You.

DOUBLE
DISPLACEMENT
REACTIONS

Behold, the Lamb of God who takes away the sin of the world! John 1:29

For by grace you have been saved through faith. Ephesians 2:8

As far as the east is from the west, so far has He removed our transgressions from us. Psalm 103:12

I, even I, am the one who wipes out your transgressions for My own sake; and I will not remember your sins. Isaiah 43:25

In a double displacement reaction two compounds react with each other to produce two new compounds. The positive ion of one compound trades places with the positive ion of the second compound and recombines with the negative ion of the other compound. For example, solutions of lead nitrate and sodium iodide can be mixed together to produce a double displacement reaction. The lead and the sodium are the positive ions. They will recombine with the opposite negative ions to produce sodium nitrate and lead iodide. As with all chemical reactions, new substances with new and different properties must be formed. In the case of double displacement reactions one of the new substances will be an insoluble solid, a gas or water. The solid, known as a precipitate, can be filtered out. The gas will form bubbles that rise and escape. The water can be boiled away. The reaction cannot reverse itself because the second compound has been removed. The other new substance is then left behind in the container. Lead nitrate and sodium iodide form colorless solutions. The lead iodide produced after they are mixed is a bright yellow solid which will settle quickly to the bottom of the container. The mixture can be poured through a filter. The sodium nitrate passes through but the lead iodide is trapped and removed.

The salvation experience is like a double displacement reaction. All people are by nature sinners. Just as a chemical compound cannot change itself, so people cannot change their sinful ways by themselves. We are bonded to sin for life unless we enter into a reaction with God and His grace. In this reaction God exchanges His grace for our sin. The whole purpose of Jesus' coming to Earth was to take our sin upon Himself so that we might become new creatures. When we give Jesus our sin, God gives us His grace. He gives it abundantly so that the reaction is complete. Our sin is completely removed. Like the solid that settles out, or the gas that bubbles away in the chemical reaction, Jesus permanently removes the sinful nature in the spiritual reaction. We trade our old life without Christ for a life with Christ. The old life is gone forever. God takes our sin, separates it from us, "as far as the east is from the west", and because it is no longer in the container where the reaction took place, He remembers it no more. That means the sin-grace reaction cannot reverse itself. Once the transaction is made, the change is permanent. We cannot change our grace bond any more than we can change our sin bond. Salvation is eternal!

Lord, thank You for providing the necessary ingredients for the permanent removal of my sin.

CATALYSTS

Jesus said to them, "With men this is impossible, but with God all things are possible." Matthew 19:26

..."for apart from Me you can do nothing." John 15:5

Catalysts are substances that are necessary in order for certain chemical reactions to take place, but which are not used up in the reactions. They play an active role in the reactions, sometimes actually becoming a part of an intermediate step of the total reaction process. The decomposition of hydrogen peroxide using iodine is an example of this. Iodine actually combines with some of the oxygen in hydrogen peroxide and then gives it up, so that water and oxygen are the final products. All of the iodine present at the beginning of the reaction is recovered at the end of the reaction. Other times catalysts act as an attractive surface, allowing the reactants to come close together, to increase their chances of reacting. In catalytic converters platinum and palladium act at high temperatures to finish the breakdown of the incomplete burning of gasoline by allowing the products to combine with oxygen. All catalysts act to speed up the rate of the reaction. Organic catalysts, called enzymes, often increase reaction rates by a million times or more. Chemical reactions in living things require the presence of enzymes, such as digestive enzymes, which are necessary for the existence of life itself.

Spiritual changes come about in much the same way. God has always worked as a catalyst. He is a necessary part of all spiritual activity. In Old Testament times He often functioned as the initiator of reactions. He gave barren women children He would later use for the building of His chosen people. He stepped into the middle of Israel's battles to bring about victories. He even acted to quickly destroy people who were intent on slowly destroying themselves. In the New Testament Jesus became God's catalyst on earth. By always doing exactly what God wanted Him to do He continued to bring to completion God's plan for the world. He stepped into the middle of sin and actually became sin on the cross so that the salvation of men could be perfected. He acted to allow men to do what they could never do by themselves, receive forgiveness for their sins. Today the Holy Spirit is the active catalyst in the world. He is the initiator of all spiritual reactions. He acts to make people realize their need for God. He points Christians in the direction God is working. He clears the path for them to join God in His work. Best of all, God is never "used up." He is I AM. What He was He will always be.

As Christians we are catalysts. We function as the second type of catalyst by attracting others to us so that God can complete the change in their lives. When non-Christians come into our presence they are drawn close to the Holy Spirit's presence so that they are more likely to hear Him speaking. When non-Christians come into our presence they should want to complete the reaction. They should want to make the change, to become new and different persons by combining with Jesus. What awesome responsibility, what a great privilege we have to be catalysts for God's work.

Lord, thank You for doing for us what we can not do for ourselves. Help us to realize how dependent we are on You.

CHEMICAL
EQUILIBRIUM

*I know your deeds, that you are neither cold or hot;
...so because you are lukewarm...I will spit you
out of My mouth. Those whom I love, I reprove
and discipline; be zealous therefore, and repent.
Revelation 3:15, 16, 19*

When a chemical reaction takes place new substances are formed. They will have new properties different from the properties of the substances that existed before the reaction took place. Ideally, none of the original substances will remain at the end of the reaction process. Some reactions will go to completion and not be able to reverse themselves, but many reactions are reversible. Some of the products will separate and re-form as the original reactants. When the speed of formation of the products and re-formation of the reactants is the same then chemical equilibrium is reached. An example of this process is the reaction of mercury (II) oxide. If it is placed in a closed container and heated the oxide will begin to separate into mercury and oxygen, but when the heat is reduced the two elements will begin to recombine into mercury (II) oxide. Eventually the amounts of the three substances will be equal in the container, and the reaction will be in equilibrium. In some chemical changes the forward reaction will nearly be complete before the reverse reaction reaches the same speed. Other reactions barely get started when the reverse reaction occurs at the same speed.

Since the purpose of chemical reactions is to get a product that is more useful than the reactants, chemical equilibrium is a detrimental process. Chemists overcome the problem by increasing the forward speed of the reaction through the use of catalysts, increasing the temperature or changing the surface area or the concentration of a substance. The only way to absolutely assure reaction completion is to remove one of the substances in the reaction.

A Christian is an example of a person who has entered into a chemical reaction with Christ. A new creature with new and different properties is formed, but because of the human sin nature, the reaction does not go to completion. There is always the pull backward into the old nature, the desire to be what he used to be. There is also the complacency that develops when he feels like he is doing well enough to be liked by everyone and to offend no one. God has provided the means to overcome the problem of Christian equilibrium. Sometimes He sends trials as a means of discipline. Other times He speaks through His Word. When a Christian becomes aware of his stagnation, he can remove himself from his environment by changing the amount of time he spends with God in prayer, in Bible study, and in relationships with other Christians. God intends for the Christian to have a reaction with Him that goes as nearly to completion as possible in this world.

Chemical reactions that go to completion are hints of what is to come. One day, God will come and remove sin entirely from the world. Then the reaction between Christ and man will go to completion and a new, perfect creature will be the only product.

Lord, I want to be the pure product You have in mind for me to be. Do what You need to do to get me to that condition.

NUCLEAR
CHANGES

In reference to your former manner of life, you lay aside the old self, which is being corrupted in accordance with the lusts of deceit, and that you be renewed in the spirit of your mind, and put on the new self, which in the likeness of God has been created in righteousness and holiness of the truth.
Ephesians 4:22-24

Nuclear changes are those changes that occur within the nucleus of an atom. Atoms that undergo nuclear changes are said to be unstable. This instability is a result of an imbalance in the ratio of protons to neutrons, the two particles that make up the nucleus. In ordinary atoms the numbers of protons and neutrons are approximately the same. The most common form of instability is an overabundance of neutrons. The binding energy of the nucleus of an unstable atom is not enough to hold it together. It will undergo nuclear changes; that is, it will release particles from the nucleus. It will give off as many particles as is necessary to achieve stability. A nuclear change always results in a change in the identity of the atom. It begins as an unstable atom of one element and ends as a stable atom of another element.

As Christians, we often are like unstable atoms. We hold on to sinful thoughts and deeds. We continue to do the things we did before Jesus came into our lives. We are at odds with ourselves, and with other Christians.

Jesus acts as the binding energy within Christians, but He will not agree to bind those attitudes and behaviors that are not Christ-like. As long as we try to hang on to them we will not be able to function as Christians, just as unstable atoms do not function as ordinary atoms. We must be willing to release our sins. Jesus is not holding them to us. He wants us to let them go. When we do let go, we will begin to change into someone new and different. Our goal should and must be to change until there is nothing left that Jesus refuses to bind. Then the nucleus of each of us will contain only those attitudes and behaviors that Jesus finds pure, lovely, and acceptable in His sight.

> *Lord, I want to be pure, and lovely, and acceptable in Your sight. Help me to want to release from my life everything that is keeping me from being a stable Christian.*

CRYSTAL
GROWTH

But grow in the grace and knowledge of our Lord and Savior Jesus Christ. 2 Peter 3:18

Solid chemical compounds exist in crystalline form. The atoms of solids are so close together that they are attracted in a way that results in a regular repeating pattern or shape. There are thousands of different substances with distinctive crystal patterns. We see them in gemstones and snowflakes, in the salt and sugar we use daily, and in the rock and soil of the earth. They are all very different from one another in their color, shape, use, and size. The color, shape, and use are a result of the particular kind of atoms with which each crystal is made. But the size of all is a result of one common factor, the amount of time the crystal is allowed to grow. The longer the crystal is in the proper environment, the larger it will grow. If it is removed from the environment, or if the environment itself changes, then growth ceases.

This idea is easily illustrated through an experiment with growing sugar crystals. A small "seed" sugar crystal is suspended in a concentrated sugar solution. The longer it is left undisturbed in the solution the larger it will become. If the solution is allowed to evaporate rapidly the crystals formed will be small. If the solution becomes contaminated with impurities, the original crystal may become covered with them until it is totally obscured.

As new Christians we are like seed crystals. We have our own distinct crystalline patterns, those characteristics that make us unlike anyone else. Each of us is a unique individual possessing special qualities given to us by God himself. But all of us, like crystals, have something in common. Our growth will be determined by the length of time we remain in an environment conducive to growth. If we limit the amount of time we spend in a Christian environment, we limit the amount we grow. If we return to our old contaminated non-Christian world, we may become so covered with the world's impurities as to be unrecognizable as children of God. We need to submerge ourselves in Christ through prayer, Bible study, and regular participation in a Bible believing church. This, and only this, will produce the beautiful large crystals so pleasing to the eye of God.

Lord, immerse me in Christ. I want to grow in His image until I am pleasing to the eye of God.

WATER OF HYDRATION

For we are His workmanship, created in Christ Jesus for good works, which God prepared beforehand, that we should walk in them. Ephesians 2:10

For just as the body without the spirit is dead, so also faith without works is dead. James 2:26

Water that is bound to the positive and negative ions of many ionic compounds is called water of hydration. Even though it is not required for that particular compound to exist, the water plays an important part in the formation of that compound's crystalline structure, luster, and sometimes its color. For example, the bright blue crystals of copper sulfate are made of copper ions surrounded by four water molecules and sulfate ions, each with one water molecule attached. Because the water molecules are only loosely attached they can be removed. If the hydrated crystals are heated the water will be driven off. The substance that remains is still copper sulfate, but now it is a white powder. It has lost both its beautiful color and its shape. However, the addition of water to that white powder will restore the copper sulfate to its original condition.

As Christians, the works that we do are the water of hydration of our faith. Faith can exist without works just as copper sulfate can exist without water, but it is just as uninteresting to the world as the white power is to the average chemistry student. Works brighten our lives, crystallize our faith, make us beautiful, and attract the attention of some who would otherwise never be interested in our faith.

Sometimes the heat of discouragement, personal problems, job obligations, or self-centeredness serves to drive works out of our lives. Our faith becomes boring and unattractive. We stay busy and yet feel that we are accomplishing little of real value. This condition does not need to be permanent any more than the powder form of copper sulfate is permanent. The Holy Spirit is always ready to restore us to good works. After all it is He who has already prepared us for them. Let us allow Him to make our faith truly lustrous and attractive to all who see us.

Lord, show me the works You have planned for me. I want to be an interesting crystalline Christian.

ICE CRYSTALS

Wash me, and I shall be whiter than snow.
Psalm 51:7

Though your sins are as scarlet, they will be as white
as snow. Isaiah 1:18

If we walk in the light as He Himself is in the light…
the blood of Jesus His Son cleanses us from all sin.
I John 1:7

When water freezes its molecules connect to form a hollow hexagonal crystal. The oxygen side of the molecule is slightly positively charged and the hydrogen ends are slightly negative. Since opposite charges attract, the oxygen and hydrogen poles are attracted. This process results in the unique open six-sided figure. The particles will continue to connect producing an ice crystal lattice. When liquid water changes to solid water the crystalline structure is not easily observed, but when water vapor changes directly to solid the tiny hexagonal crystals are readily identified. These are known as snow crystals, and it is from these crystals that snowflakes are formed. The simplest ones are six-sided plates or columns. The complex snowflakes are made as water vapor sublimates on the corners of their facets. The formation of the crystals is dependent on the temperature and humidity factors in the clouds. Because these conditions are not stable the growing crystal shape is constantly changing. A variety of snowflake patterns are the result. In fact, it is highly probable that the saying, "no two snowflakes are alike", is true. What does remain constant is that no matter the complexity of their development, all snowflakes have six sides. Although snow appears to be an opaque white, the ice crystals of individual snowflakes are actually clear. The white color is a result of the reflection of most of the incoming light from the snow. A small amount of light is absorbed, primarily red light waves, so sometimes snow banks will have a slightly blue cast that makes them appear especially clean and pure.

Christians are like snowflakes. Each of us grows under different genetic and environmental conditions. We are unique individuals, but we all have one aspect in common. We are sinners. The hexagonal designs are representative of our sinful nature. The number six is used in scripture to indicate sin as it is one less than the number seven, the number of perfection. All people, including Christians, are less than perfect. We cannot hide our sin from God. Like snowflakes we are clear so He can see right through us. God, in love, sent His Son Jesus to cleanse us from our sin with His own blood. When we allow Him to wash us, we begin to live in His light. We reflect that light so that God sees His own light coming from us, and to Him we appear white as snow. And since we have absorbed the red blood of Christ like the snow absorbs red light, what a pure, sparkling white it is!

> *Lord, wash me. I want to reflect Your purity. Thank You for allowing us to be in Your light.*

SOLUTIONS

Even As Thou, Father, art in Me, and I in Thee, that they also may be in Us; that the world may believe that Thou didst sent Me. John 17:21

For you have died and you life is hidden with Christ in God. When Christ, who is our life, is revealed, then you also will be revealed with Him in glory. Colossians 3:3-4

A solution is a special type of mixture made of two parts. The solute is the part that is dissolved. The solvent is the part that does the dissolving. The state of matter of the solvent determines the solution types, which are named accordingly: solid solution, liquid solution, or gaseous solution. The word *dissolve* means to evenly mix so that all samples of the mixture will contain equal amounts of the solute. In the solution process, molecules of the solvent surround and separate particles of the solute. These particles of solute are the size of the molecules or ions that make up the substance. As a result they are invisible to the eye, even with a microscope. The solute has not lost its identity, but has increased its usefulness to the chemist. For example, solid sugar in a bowl does nothing; but when it becomes a part of a pitcher of tea or a bottle of carbonated drink, it makes a tasty solution. The sugar cannot be seen but is tasted. The sweetness of the drink proves it is still present.

As Christians, we are part of a special type of mixture. This is exactly what God wants us to be. We are the solutes and Jesus is the solvent. He wants to separate and surround us totally, so that we are completely and evenly mixed in Him. We will disappear from view as separate particles in the world. As a result, when others observe us they will notice Jesus first. We are called Christians because Christ is the solvent.

Just as a solute does not lose its properties in the solution process, so Christians also do not lose their characteristics. God does not want us to be identical to one another. Instead, He uses our individual personality traits for His own special purpose. We certainly would not flavor our tea with salt, and neither would we season our meat with sugar. God has a particular purpose for each of us, if we will become one with Christ and thus be usable to Him.

Lord, I want to be one with You so that others see Jesus when they look at me.

RATE OF
SOLUTION

The sacrifices of God are a broken spirit; A broken and a contrite heart, O God, Thou wilt not despise. Psalm 51:17

The Pharisee stood and was praying thus to himself, "God, I thank Thee that I am not like other people." The tax gatherer was beating his breast, saying, "God, be merciful to me, the sinner!" This man went down to his house justified rather than the other; for everyone who exalts himself shall be humbled, but he who humbles himself shall be exalted. Luke 18:11-14

The rate at which a substance dissolves depends on several factors: the temperature of the solvent, the stirring of the mixture, and the size of the particles of solute. All of these things allow the solvent to act more effectively on the solute so that it is broken down to molecular sized particles. The solvent molecules surround the molecules on the surface of the lump of solute and pull them away. The process continues until the solute particles are all separated and surrounded by the solvent molecules. Stirring the mixture and changing the temperature of the solvent are ways of changing the environment of the solute to encourage more rapid dissolving, but the rate at which the solute will dissolve is most dependent on the size of the lumps. Chemists usually break apart the lumps before they try to dissolve the solute. This increases the total surface area that is exposed to the solvent. More solvent molecules can act on more solute particles at the same time, thus shortening the dissolving time and making the solution available for use by the chemist more quickly.

As Christians, we are like the solute. The Holy Spirit is the chemist. Some Christians never allow themselves to be acted upon by the Holy Spirit. They, like the Pharisee who prayed his self-contented prayer, remain as solid lumps of chemical in a jar. They like themselves as they are, and see no need to change. Other Christians allow themselves to be placed in the solvent by the Holy Spirit, but they do not want Him to "dissolve" too much. They enter the solution process as a large lump, and only let the solvent, Jesus, act on their outermost layers. Their usefulness to God is limited as a result. A few Christians want to be used as completely as possible by God. Like the tax gatherer who, in total humility, prayed for mercy, these individuals admit to themselves and the Lord that they are useless in their original form. They let the Holy Spirit break them down so that Jesus can surround their every part. These are the Christians who become the most used by God. Sometimes God will stir us or heat us to change our environment; that is, He will adjust our circumstances to remind us of our need to be surrounded by Him completely. Just as agitation and changing particle size and temperature are positive actions taken by the chemist in the solution process, so are the spiritual stirring, breaking, and heating always positive actions taken by God, designed to make us usable.

> *Lord, be merciful to me. Forgive me for liking myself as I am. Break me; surround my every part with Your Spirit so that I can be used by You.*

EMULSIONS

And although you were formerly alienated and hostile in mind, engaged in evil deeds, yet He has now reconciled you in His fleshly body through death, in order to present you before Him holy and blameless and beyond reproach. Colossians 1:21-22

For He Himself is our peace, who made both groups into one, and broke down the barrier of the dividing wall. Ephesians 2:14

An emulsion is a special mixture of two liquids that will not ordinarily mix. One liquid is made of polar molecules, that is, molecules that have positive and negative areas because of unequal sharing of electrons between the atoms of which they are made. The other liquid is non-polar in nature; its molecules have no electrically charged areas. Under ordinary conditions these types of liquids even when shaken together, will separate quickly. Water and oil are good examples of these kinds of liquids. Water is polar while oil is non-polar. Oil and water do not mix no matter how long and hard they are shaken. As soon as the agitation stops they separate. An emulsifying agent is required to produce an emulsion. The agent has properties that allow it to come between the polar and non-polar particles and hold them together. Soap is an emulsifying agent for water and oil.

One end of the long soap molecule is polar; the other end is non-polar. Following the principle of "like dissolves like", the polar end attracts the water molecules and the non-polar end attracts the oil molecules. A few drops of soap shaken with the oil and water will cause the oil and water to appear to mix together.

As Christians, Jesus holds us, both to God the Father and to other Christians. We are sinners by nature, alienated from God, Who is perfect and holy and cannot sin. Jesus came as God in the flesh and took on our sins as His own. He was completely God and completely man at the same time. As such, He is our emulsifying agent. He stands between God and us and holds us together. The "man side" takes our sin and the "God side" presents us holy and blameless before God.

In the same way Jesus acts to aid Christians in getting along with other Christians. We do not all agree with each other about everything. We often let our differences divide us into factions who argue and fight, or who ignore each other. This animosity will continue no matter how hard we try on our own to solve our problems. All the pacts, peace treaties, and coalitions will mean nothing if God is not acting as our emulsifier. Sooner or later we will be right back where we started. Only Jesus can remedy this situation. Only by seeing other Christians through Jesus' eyes can we live in peace.

Lord, thank You for sending Jesus to be our reconciler.

SUSPENSIONS

They are not of the world, even as I am not of the world. As Thou didst send Me into the world, I also have sent them into the world. John 17:16, 18

And on that day great persecution arose against the church in Jerusalem; and they were all scattered throughout the regions of Judea and Samaria. Therefore, those who had been scattered went about preaching the word. Acts 8:1, 4

And how shall they preach unless they are sent? Just as it is written, "How beautiful are the feet of those who bring glad tidings of good things!" Romans 10:15

A suspension is a type of mixture, a physical combination of two substances. It differs from solutions, which are also mixtures, in the size of the particles. The particles are larger than the molecular sized solutes of solutions, and may even be visible to the unaided eye. They do not dissolve. They just float in the other substance that makes up the mixture. This causes a suspension to appear cloudy instead of clear like a solution. Also, because they are larger, the particles will tend to clump together and to separate from the medium with which they are mixed. Many commonly used products, from aerosols such as spray paints, to foods like salad dressings, and to medicines like milk of magnesia or that pink, bubble-gum flavored, liquid antibiotic are suspensions. They can be easily recognized as such by the phrase on the container's label, "Shake well before using." The product is useful and valuable, not because of the substance which is the suspension medium, but because of the particles which have separated from it. If the directions are not followed the suspension medium is all that will be poured or sprayed from the container. Consequently, it cannot perform as described on the product label to give satisfactory results.

As Christians, our relationship to the world is like that of the ingredients in a suspension. We are mixed in with non-Christians in our everyday lives, but we never become an integral part of the mixture. Christians should make the world cloudy; that is, our presence should be obvious. We should be to the world of today what Jesus was to the world of His day, a compassionate healer, a discerner of good and evil, an earthly image of God himself. Those who came in contact with Him knew immediately that He was not like them. They knew He had something to offer that no one else could offer.

It is not easy to float in an incompatible medium. Just as suspended particles tend to clump and separate, so do Christians tend to form their exclusive groups, effectively separating themselves from the world. The unsaved world by itself cannot fulfill the claims it makes on its label, no matter how hard it tries or how often it applies its "cure". From the earliest days of Christianity, beginning with the church in Jerusalem and the ministry of Paul, God has read His own directions and has "shaken well." Through the ages it has been the influence of godly individuals scattered by God that has brought about the positive changes in the world's attitudes and activities. Even more importantly, the preaching of God's Word has produced countless Christians in almost every nation on Earth. So, when we as Christians today find ourselves in the midst of a lost world, instead of feeling alone and sorry for ourselves, we should rejoice that God has considered us useful, valuable, and able to perform as described on His label. How beautiful it is to have the privilege of carrying God's message to a lost and dying world!

Lord, shake me. I want the world to see You.

STONES

Jesus said, "If these (people) become silent, the stones will cry out!" His words are more profound than anyone who heard them that day could have imagined. I believe that when He said the stones would cry out He meant it literally. God most certainly can cause the rocks to shout out and speak of His glory. God's creation will always give Him praise. I believe, however, that Jesus' statement has a much deeper meaning than that.

You have read in this book of another way the stones can speak, through their physical and chemical properties and reactions. Jesus knew they could talk that way. After all, He created them and knows everything about them. It is amazing how much the stones have to say to the world. They continually point to God and praise Him for Who He is. As long as the universe exists they will shout out His mighty works. They will extol His majesty. They will cry to us to believe in Him and accept His Son as our Savior. They will admonish us to do the same.

This leads to a third interpretation of this scripture, that Jesus meant the Christian community would cry out when His own people rejected Him. He knew the Holy Spirit would lead Peter to call us "living stones". He says we "are being built up as a spiritual house for a holy priesthood, to offer up spiritual sacrifices acceptable to God through Jesus Christ." (1 Peter 2:5) Jesus told his disciples to go out to the entire world preaching, making disciples, and teaching them to obey His commandments. It is no wonder then that the rocks tell us that we are to spread the word about God's plan for the salvation of the world. They are just repeating Jesus' words to us. Through His strength and power we, too, can shout out and speak of His glory.

If the non-living stones can cry out, how can we, who are alive in Christ, do otherwise?

Printed in the United States
By Bookmasters